ZEN 2.0

Eastern Solutions for the Western World

www.zenrevolution.com

To Steve Jobs
(in memoriam)

ZEN 2.0

Eastern Solutions for the Western World

ISBN 978-1-300-19235-0 *(by lulu)*

APPROACH

PREFACE

Firstly, thank you so much for reading this. It is just a first step on the road to joining the Zen Revolution. I must confess at this point that the version of Zen contained in this book is my own, home-made, one. It is by no means extreme and is intended to be compatible with a more Westernised way of thinking. It will not treat you harshly to teach you its valuable lessons. You won't have to throw your Smartphone down the toilet and flush it away. It won't expect you to walk out from your job or compel you to give up your mortgage payments just because it disagrees with the concept. You certainly won't arrive at your next business meeting dressed in an orange robe and with a shaved head.

My approach to Zen retains all of the most beneficial aspects of our Western culture that have an association with it and its understanding of harmony in all things. This incorporates a peaceful co-existence with our outer environment and inner self, the value of tranquility, appreciating the simplicity of natural forms and the beautiful clarity of ideas.

For the realization of my approach I have permitted myself to combine the most appropriate elements of Hinduism, Taoism, Confucianism, Buddhism and other Eastern belief systems. I have done this to reveal the practical disciplines contained within all of them that are the most valuable to us. They are usually diluted in a confusion of vague philosophical storytelling or corny platitudes.

I completed the process of harvesting the profoundest ideas to be found within these various religions. Then, I brought them together. The methodology I arrived at became christened the Zen Revolution. It became a system of specific philosophical actions that had been stripped down to their bare rhetorical essentials. By applying the practices of the Zen Revolution to daily life the clear ideological benefits within ancient culture can be integrated easily into our modern, Western, one.

Throughout this whole creative process I have enjoyed the support of several individuals with their own unique connections to Eastern culture and belief. They have all helped me tremendously in the process of adaptation. In particular I should like to express my appreciation for the assistance provided to me by Bernard, a French-born Buddhist monk. He left his job as an engineer at a major telecommunications company during that terrible recent period in France characterized by bullying and multiple suicides. Bernard knows better than anyone the dual importance of the world of work and the world of worship. His advice and good counsel have been critical to the completion of this work.

The main intention is to reveal the benefits to the Western life in general and our own personal lives in particular that the path of Zen can provide. The advantages apply as much to our professional lives as our personal ones. Although many of the examples I give relate to the business world, the lessons they provide are directly transferable to our private lives.

Indeed, my own experiences illustrate everything that this book is seeking to address. I don't wear orange robes or have a closely-shaved head. There's no need for the latter because I'm already going bald. I have the latest model of iPhone and I enjoy a life that includes all the comforts that the modern world can provide. On a personal level, I have what must seem from the outside to be an enviable life with a wonderful family and a great many good friends. My less enjoyable experiences have been focused more in my working life. That is not to say my career hasn't been successful or satisfying, it has. The sense of dissatisfaction has been found instead in negative interactions with other people. Bad energy can persist in a working space, cling to you and drain your energy and enthusiasm away. Sometimes my friendly greetings and casual inquiries to work colleagues about their wellbeing were neutralized immediately. Their depressing replies and long dramatic stories about their illnesses, arguments and issues merely added to my stress levels and kept me awake at night. They never seemed to exceed my natural tolerance level though.

To be honest, there was nothing about my life that I could really complain about. Nevertheless, a few years ago I began to feel that something vital was missing. If there had been a specific problem like not having a partner, having an unfulfilling job or suffering financial problems it would have been easy to attribute this sense of lack to any of those. There was nothing wrong though. Nothing at all. I was perfectly at peace and content. I still felt increasingly uneasy and I wondered why. I had to look deeper.

That was the time when I delivered myself into the hands of the Zen masters. Slowly, but surely, I began to sense the truth. Personal happiness can only be achieved when you choose the path that you need to follow and just surrender to it. Being conscious of my personal path was, without doubt, a major revelation to me. It was also a turning point in my life. I am the first to admit that the changes that I made seemed minimal, after all my life already makes me happy, so why make radical changes? On the other hand, the changes were deep enough, and, although subtle, significant enough to change me. I have undergone a personal revolution - a Revolution Zen. Since then, I never have to beep my horn at anyone when I'm in my car, I sleep the whole night through and I'm always in a good mood. We could say that my life is practically the same as before, only calmer and more balanced: in short, happier.

So now, every morning when I wake up, the first thing I do is read the obituaries in the newspaper. If my name isn't there I tell myself, "Today will be a great day."

Bearing this in mind, and taking into account my greater experience and learning, this book, I hope, will shed more light on the road that everyone has to walk on in solitude. It is our own private path. The real challenge, simply put, is to proceed towards our destiny, the one we build each day with every one of our own decisions.

Welcome to Zen

BRIEF NOTES ABOUT ZEN

In Zen there is no objective reality. What we perceive as being real is merely a projection of our consciousness. If that is the case then the payment of taxes must be a very strange part of our imagination. We can spend hours in meditation, watching our mind and controlling our breathing but as Lao Tzu has written: "*the world is governed by the things that are ongoing*". That means taxes as well. We have two choices. We can employ a clever accountant to build an elaborate tax avoidance mechanism for us and hope that it works or we can submit the relevant document and just pay up. No philosophy yet devised can save us from a fine for late payment.

It may appear as though I'm trivializing Zen by saying this but that couldn't be further from the truth. Zen originated in antiquity but it is also fun, encourages spontaneity and remains earthy. It is true that, from our Westernised perspective, the rituals that originated in Asia (Japanese Zen has its roots in both India and China) can seem formal and solemn. The strength of Zen resides in the simplicity of its foundations and not the earnestness of its rituals.

The cultural roots of Western culture and its Asian equivalent are so different that, in spite of the increasing uniformity brought about by globalization, the innate truths of one or the other still don't translate well. Zen, as presented here, is a version that has been tailored to fit the Western mentality. In a sense it has been decaffeinated. We cannot pretend to understand it unless both sides adapt to each others needs for clarity. Zen seems like a contradiction in the mundane materialism of the hyper-accelerated business world of the West. The art of Bonsai doesn't seem to fit into the same era as data analysis and the construction of a successful business strategy.

In the final decades of the twentieth century, the increasing stresses of daily living and the demands and dissatisfactions within our

Western consumer society led to a collapse in spiritual values. We began to look Eastward for a model that offered a greater spiritual reality. What started in restaurants with spring rolls and sushi spread with the public interest in Yoga, Tai Chi, Aikido and Feng-Shui. Even the bedroom wasn't immune from the effect of the Kama Sutra and Tantric Sex. The Eastern influence is here to stay because, despite its ancient origins, it has breathed new life into a Western model that was too rigid and fixed to reinvent itself.

But how does Zen fits into all this? And more specifically, what the hell is Zen?

Despite having its origins in Buddhism, the truth is that Zen isn't really a religious doctrine or value system at all. Neither is it a dogma or something we, with our corseted mentality, can catalogue easily. The inability to classify it is not, in and of itself, a problem. In the same way we know what an orgasm is even though we cannot adequately describe the sensations involved. We can list the chemical processes involved in it and explain that by stimulating the genitals we release Oxytocin but its essence will always elude academic understanding.

Continuing with the example of the orgasm, we find the core element of Zen in our own experiences. Given that the concept of Zen is so intangible, no one can transmit it to us. This means that we must reach it for ourselves and fortunately, it's a lot closer than we think. All that is required is a little push to find it.

However, the lack of definition of the concept does not prevent us from identifying Zen with some very distinctive features, such as a taste for simplicity of forms and concepts, harmony within the environment, balanced ideas and inner peace. These are all concepts of Zen but are not, in any case, exclusive to it. Many other moral constructs (religions, philosophies, etc.) use them and they are the foundations of basic common sense. In fact, like any great universal idea, in practically every culture we can find popular proverbs that somehow reflect these universal values that coincide with our basic human nature.

At first, it may be the case that some of these concepts seem contradictory (for example: meditating and acting, thinking without thinking,...). However, gradually everything will fall into place. In short, in spite of the reference to Zen that appears in the title of this book, the essence is nothing but a proposal to make the most of these universal values that are in full force all around the world. Especially in the "Here and Now" of the Western world.

The truth is that, somehow, Zen (with the values it represents) is fashionable. This is so because the values of Zen respond to a demand for spirituality and values in Western society today. However, it is difficult to go deep enough into Zen using a traditional approach. Not because of its complexity (because it is very simple), but because it is impossible to manage it in a way that is compatible with the rest of our realities. There are four main factors that prevent this:

1. The lack of specificity. Zen stories and the lessons they contain are inspiring and cause you to reflect. The things that we read into them can be hard to apply to real life.

2. Time pressures. We never have sufficient time. The idea that devoting more of our lives to the ongoing process of enlightenment and on hours spent in meditation to help us save time seems unlikely. There are always things that need doing.

3. Lack of realism. To redesign the way we think is fine in theory but the circumstances of our lives are more resistant to change. Our obligations, whether professional or personal, cannot be transformed so easily. Selling our possessions and moving to a Buddhist retreat sounds blissful but it's not what we really crave

4. Lack of role models. There is a cliched image of the practicing Buddhist that puts us off listening to them. We find it hard to identify with their lives and so their valuable teachings about Eastern philosophy don't inspire us.

It is clear that this image puts up a barrier to the fuller understanding of Zen in our society. Our reluctance to embrace it is a direct consequence of our day to day Western pragmatism. That is a common point of view.

The truth is that to discover Zen, we needn't have to begin from a state of unhappiness, restlessness or lack of fulfillment. Neither do we need to be high-flying business executives. We don't have to wait for a spiritual revelation, a physical breakdown or existential crisis either before we consider trading our conventional life for one in a monastery instead. It isn't required to get up at the crack of dawn or undergo formal sacrifices of any kind. Don't forget that Zen monasteries are no picnic. It makes no sense to turn back the clock by 3000 years just to be authentic.

An interest in Zen in our society has led to a rapid increase in Yoga centers and meditation classes. This can only be a good thing as they can only increase self-awareness. It is surprising that some attendees achieve a state of enlightenment after only one evening session. It took Buddha himself so much longer. One must be a little skeptical. It's incredible to imagine that turning up to class, doing a few breathing exercises and listening to four bells is all it takes to become realized.

So, Zen, provided it is clear of any hint of “dime-store philosophy” has a great deal to offer everyone. We are all looking for something more. This doesn't have to mean finding peace of mind in the spiritual or metaphysical sense. It could just be confirmation that we are fulfilling our destiny according to our own intuition.

Unhappiness leads to us not feeling that inner peace and, in fact, is the main cause of many visits received by psychologists. However, happiness does not have a psychological origin, but is spiritual instead. Of course, both psychologists and psychiatrists do an extraordinary job treating people who suffer from real mental problems, but in many other cases the problem is purely spiritual: the distance between depression and a simple personal feeling of emptiness is huge. However the limits can sometimes appear to be fuzzy and ambiguous for the person who is living it in first person.

Therefore, despite not acknowledging another significance than that of humans, Zen is based on certain elements of spirituality that always have the ultimate goal of achieving personal balance and harmony with the environment, that eventually leads to inner peace.

Not only the kind of inner peace that is associated with Zen, but also with all the elements that are present in Eastern culture.

However, this book has been written by Westerners for Westerners. Using techniques designed for implementation in our own Western world, but with a foundation that gives off a subtle aroma of incense and lotus flowers.

WORK NOTES

If you just skim through the pages of this book you will derive little benefit from it. The understanding that Zen is a unique path that is built from the experiments of the individual is vital in this context. I recommend that you study each of the lessons, meditate on them and apply them directly to the reality of your own life and circumstances. What makes YOU happy? What's missing from YOUR life? Who are YOUR friends?

There are also recommended texts and exercises throughout the text, as well as those that appear at the end of the book. You can also find many more on www.RevolucionZen.com

Towards the back of the book, you will find some blank pages where you can make notes on any aspects that have attracted your attention, or things you wish to reflect back on. You can also use this space to jot down your own ideas or any personal concerns that arise during the time of reading.

Therefore, although it is clear that this book could be read in one go, it is interesting to consider a more leisurely re-read, page by page, idea by idea. During each one you can make notes, underline things, do some of the proposed exercises, or just take a few moments to reflect on an idea. For this you can – and you should – take all the time you need. The next page in this book will still be in the same place as it is today. Really.

PRINCIPLES

WHAT IS SUCCESS?

Success is a subjective concept. We tend to relate it to those things that produce a sense of well-being in us, satisfaction in our accomplishments and quantifiable rewards. We all understand what makes us happy as individuals so our own ideas of success are also unique to us. Happiness is the ultimate goal in life.

It is a human characteristic to try and achieve success in as short a time as possible. Zen teaches us that our own anxiety to be successful quickly will thwart us, over and over again, in achieving that objective.

The real world teaches us that there are no shortcuts. Achievements are made by walking a path of many steps. Tao tells us that these steps can comprise work, sacrifice and making decisions. In between those major steps are intermediate ones on which we must build realistic ambitions. These goals must be clear and concrete and not based on monetary gain. For example, we would envisage selling 100 units first before we focus on the $10,000 profit. We must be dedicated to our efforts first. Our sales will not increase by a projected 22% if we fail to set down a structure to enable it.

If we focus upon these intermediate steps and carry them out as best we can, then we can anticipate a job well done and then eventual success.

In some cases we apply ourselves as we should but the effort goes unrewarded. If we review the stages we took from the beginning we may find that there was no error in our decision-making. What evidence did we base that decision on? We could have applied a valid market study, set down a viable business plan or initiated a timely corporate restructuring process. If they were judged to increase the probability of success then why didn't they work?

It's clear that we will only succeed if we made the right decision that would have lit the wick. How can we know what the right decision is? What is it that can ignite our intuition so that we know which choice to make?

NOTES

SUCCESS IS ENLIGHTENMENT

Success has a metaphysical component that defies rational explanation.

There are predictable elements that increase the probability of personal success. These can include training, hard work and self-sacrifice. They can't guarantee the ideal outcome. These skills are taught to us from a young age. They begin at home, proceed through school and reach their conclusion in business academies and universities. If the secret to success was contained in this process then we would all have it.

This must mean that there is something else happening that can't be taught or described but must be felt or experienced in a unique way. In some way, on the road to eventual success, some people perceive a truth that eludes everyone else. Their understanding is deepened and their unique sensitivity in that moment elevates them above all others. This is enlightenment and it is the very essence of Zen.

We have all known someone who seemed like a bad bet for success who, nevertheless, seemed to achieve it anyway. This didn't just confuse us or make us jealous of their achievement. We would have attributed it to good fortune. The successful individual might have dismissed it as being the result of hard work or simple skill.

Eventually we intuit that something else was going on in the background. Some light inside them guided their way.

If we really want to pursue success we must create the conditions within us that will facilitate the light of inspiration. It will reveal the path that is meant for us and it will lead us forward. If the notion of enlightenment is too philosophical then we can rely upon the word intuition instead. Other synonyms like smell or a sixth sense are just as good. More important than our comfort with the idea is the way we can help to bring it about.

NOTES

TAKE A LOOK INSIDE

"The only Zen you find on tops of mountains is the Zen you bring there".

RM Pirsig

As we have seen when talking about Success, the light that illuminates the right decisions comes from within each person. Its existence isn't rational or conscious but instead has a more intuitive focus. It is similar to when, out of the blue, we remember something that happened years ago for no apparent reason, or suddenly we remember that clients name that we had forgotten at yesterday's meeting. However, this does not mean that it isn't a fully mental process. It is true that the process flows in a natural way, but it is our mind that ultimately dictates the decisions we make. For this reason we must help our minds to think clearly so that it proposes the best decisions for us.

The ultimate goal of Zen, as we have seen, is to create conditions that allow our minds to be comfortable enough so that everything flows freely in a non-forced way. It is the light that illuminates our decisions.

In short, we can spend hours mulling over any decision that we make. We can talk and ask for opinions from other people or use infinity of decision-making tools that could include anything from plucking a daisy to calculating the Return of Investment. The crystal ball is no longer in fashion. However, sooner or later we will have to make a decision. We must see it clearly for ourselves, trust our own instinct and say "go ahead". The Answer will not magically appear out of nowhere. It is difficult to consider all the variables at stake when making a specific decision. Besides, each variable would lead to a different answer and there is never a single answer. The only valid answer is our own one. So, we have no choice but to look within, take a deep breath and then move one step forward. If we are able to generate the conditions that allow our mind to see clearly, our own answer will be the right one.

NOTES

FREE YOUR MIND

To ensure that our minds are working to their full potential, and that they can be enlightened, we must create the right circumstances.

Zen establishes a set of useful principles that can help us free our minds. The first stage in the process is to recognize the path we need to follow and then resolve to do so. Only then can anticipate the release. To be able to do this we must admit to ourselves that something restrains us. Sometimes that initial realization can be elusive.

Tao-sin asked of his master Seng-ts'an:
"How do I free myself?"
"What is it that imprisons you?" the master asked.
"Nothing" the student replied.
"Then how can you escape if there is nothing to escape from?" the master inquired.

We must free ourselves from everything that restrains us, suppresses our thoughts and clouds our vision. It might be the fear that a personal project might fail. It can be the overwhelming stress caused by an exhaustive agenda or the preconceived ideas about how we might manage a potential client. We could be weighed down by the threat of a failed quality assessment or the fear that our line of credit won't be extended and that our short-term cash-flow will dry up. Threats to liquidity are a real and present danger as anyone who has run a company with tight resources will understand. Nevertheless, we cannot let our minds be conditioned by fear. Even when we control our anxieties, the effort needed to do so reduces our ability to make progress.

The first step on the path to Zen is to reflect on exactly what constrains you. Then -and only then- can you compartmentalize it in your mind and work on it. You cannot expect to identify the problem and resolve it after five minutes of consideration. The issue will be more complex than that and it will take longer than you think to moderate its effect. The important thing is to recognize the underlying cause that limits your mind and accept that it will be a work-in-progress to free yourself from it completely.

NOTES

HERE AND NOW

The best tool that there is to help free the mind is our acceptance that all we have is the present. In Zen there exists a single point in time and that is simply the here and now. It's the only reality that is affected by our actions.

Any other fanciful notions of alternate realities like space and time, past and future are distractions that can disrupt our equilibrium and, in the worst cases, cripple our minds.

To keep our minds tranquil we must eliminate any and all unnecessary interruptions either real or imagined. This also applies to those things that cause stress in our lives. Anything that prevents us from focusing will just cast shadows across our path to enlightenment.

Don't waste time worrying about a business that might have failed in the past. The positive outcome is that you've learned how NOT to do something. Nor should you get stressed out about the same problem over and over again. Instead, you should focus on the solution. The most wasteful thing we can do is theorize about problems that may or may not even occur. This is like being seduced by your own thought processes. Avoid fantasizing about your idyllic future when your idea has taken off. Imagining the resulting earnings is even worse. Think instead about every hour of hard work it will take to realize this outcome. In the present, you'll need to maintain your perspective, work hard and keep on developing your idea into something that people want. By all means reflect on the past and maintain hopes for the future, but remember that it is in the now that we find the foundation on which to build our future security.

In the case of the spatial factor concerning the Here, the reality is even more evident. We should only care about what is happening in the physical space of the Here, given that it is the only thing that we have a direct influence over. It is clear that with technology, the concept of the Here is very different from the original Here found in Zen. However, the essence is the same. You should only worry about those things that you have a direct influence on because, in one way or another, it is at your fingertips.

NOTES

MEDITATE

Meditation is the essence of Zen, and it consists of the consecration of our minds in the act of thinking, without thinking. Something that almost seems impossible!

So, we should just try to be serene, calm and relaxed, let our thoughts flow in peace without stressing ourselves out by trying to find an answer. It's about finding peace for your mind, and the answer will then appear spontaneously.

For this, we must aim to create the appropriate circumstances for such a process. Naturally, we can have fleeting thoughts in the middle of a boring meeting or in the waiting lounge of an airport. For our mind to achieve its full potential, we should make time to be in a relaxing space, without any kind of distractions or interruptions. It isn't necessary to set up a sanctuary or to be five hours in trance or anything of the sort. Just being in a tranquil environment is enough. A place where we can dedicate a few minutes a day to take care of our main productive asset: our mind.

Meditating, in any case, has little to do with the pre-conceived idea of deep thinking. In fact, it is the total opposite.

Thinking is the conscious rational process of assessing the variables involved in making a decision: from our knowledge or experience, we look at the pros and cons of hiring enthusiastic juniors or seniors with contacts, to maintain a certain price campaign based on results...

In contrast, meditation is the intuitive process of letting all the variables in our mind to settle and take shape, until we suddenly realize what the right decision is. In fact, it is an unconscious process of spontaneous organization of information which has certain similarities to the neuronal disconnection that occurs during sleep (hence the term "sleeping on it"). In any case, Meditation is the exact opposite of thinking: it is non-thinking. In order to “not-think”, there are two alternatives: you can either leave your mind blank (which is very difficult), or deal with releasing activities that keep us busy and distracted from any particular concern (a game of chess, reading a book ...)

NOTES

OPEN YOUR MIND

"Do not seek the truth; only cease to cherish opinions"

Seng-T'San

To encourage your mind to discover the answer that will lead to enlightenment you must remove any preconceived ideas and then allow reality to flow around you freely. In doing so, you must avoid making judgments and not attempt to analyze the world at a conscious level. The mind must be protected from the influence of outer concerns and itself.

The mental process has a cognitive phase in which we perceive the nature of things and a deductive phase in which we draw conclusions from them. We should, instead, allow our subconscious to do the work for us. If we relax and accept all the possibilities we will see that they are endless.

To have an open mind means, ultimately, to accept the nature of reality without filtering it through our own preconceptions.

In this way, a potential client deserves 100% of our attention without part of it being used to examine his wristwatch to decide whether it's of high quality or not. We can never know their exact motivations for purchasing it unless they tell us of course. It's like going fishing.

Until you pull the rod up you will never see what might be on the end of the line. This metaphor could be applied to the beginning of any relationship, whether it lasts for a single night or continues on for a lifetime.

Another way to look at it would be to imagine a competition in which the top prize would be the award of a prestigious technical project. If we say that "our competition has three times the financial resources in R & D than we have" then factually, that might be the case. The subjectivity of assuming that they will win because of that fact will cause us more damage than their whole roster of patents ever will.

Therefore, if we open our mind to objective reality and avoid the trap of judging the world around us according to our preconceptions, the limitations we set ourselves fall away. What seem to be unbreakable barriers will be revealed as being made of paper. They can be brushed aside easily if we move forward with firmness and determination.

NOTES

DO ONE THING AT A TIME

To unburden your mind, and so be better able to focus on discovering the answer that will enlighten you, we should concentrate on one mental process at a time. If you need to think then do it. If you write, make that the only task. If you talk, do that exclusively.

As has been noted when referring to the Here and Now, the existence of a definitive present would appear to place a clear limitation upon us. The fact is, that we can only do a single thing at one time.

This apparent restriction actually contains some useful concepts with reference to personal, and business, organization. These include time management and resource optimization.

All of this is derived from a simple observation. Human beings, especially male, are not multi-tasking in a way that is beneficial to the end result. Our objective reality resembles the efficiency of a computer that is overwhelmed by an excessive amount of demands. The more we ask it to do the slower anything is achieved until, finally, the system crashes. The only solution to that eventuality is to turn off and re-boot. Then, by prioritizing only the essential tasks we can begin again and achieve results.

Zen offers a simple approach that is related directly to common sense. We can only do one thing at a time if we hope to do it well. It is a fallacy to imagine that by doing a lot of things simultaneously we are actually making progress.

In fact, there are several modern time management techniques taught in seminars at some of the finest business schools, as well as countless software solutions (from simple to complex scheduling program tasks as well as project systems). But in order to have the peace required to do just one thing at a time, is first and foremost a mental attitude.

In addition, complying with this rule is also a sign of respect for yourself. Nobody likes it when others interrupt us when we are busy doing something, so why do we interrupt ourselves constantly?

NOTES

URGENT AND IMPORTANT

When ordering the tasks before focusing on just one, the classic mistake is to prioritize the urgent before the important. We often forget that the urgent can perhaps prevent us from failure at a given time. However, on the road to success, it is necessary to focus on the important.

In addition, the urgent is in itself purely reactive, and if we let ourselves be drawn into the reactive spiral, we risk becoming troubleshooters unable to direct our own lives. It could be that we see ourselves deprived of the objective that creates the distance. Or we could imagine that we are heading towards a path of constant distractions that separate us from the path of liberations that we aim to follow.

Today, advances in information technology and communications add an element of distortion which the Zen masters did not encounter during their time. The concept of the Here and Now has become relative and we have the tools to reach it all. Of course, the misuse of powerful weapons is incredibly dangerous, but in this case, the omnipresence of communication can become a constant attack on our need for peace, tranquility and meditation. This doesn't mean you should throw your Smartphone out the window in the midst of the

21st century; however, we should turn it off from time to time or even leave it at home if we go out for a walk.

There is a Zen proverb from 2,000 years ago, attributed to Buddha himself, that says: "*Do not check your work email on a Friday evening just before leaving. You will review your inbox on Monday*". Of course it wasn't exactly like this given that there was no email during the time of Buddha. However, if it had existed, it surely would have been something similar.

Basically, whether you answer the email today or not, the sun will still rise for you tomorrow and for the person who has sent it.

NOTES

IT ALL DEPENDS...

Many years ago, a horse managed to escape from the property of a Japanese farmer.

"What bad luck you had!" exclaimed his neighbors when they heard of it, "It depends" -the farmer replied..

The missing horse returned to the farmer the very next day. It was joined by six young, and beautiful, wild horses of great value.

"You've had such good luck" exclaimed the neighbors when they heard of it. "It depends" the farmer replied impassively.

That very same day, the farmer's son chose to mount one of the wild horses. He was thrown off and fell to the ground, breaking one of his legs.

"What very bad luck you had" exclaimed the neighbors once more. The farmer replied again impassive "It depends"

After another week had passed, the armies of the Emperor passed through the village. They sought to recruit all able-bodied young men into their ranks. The farmer son, nursing his broken leg, was spared the duty of going to war.

The farmer's neighbors congratulated him. "You've had good luck", they exclaimed. "It depends" -he replied impassively.

The next stage in unburdening your mind of fear and anxiety is to spare yourself the confusion of wondering whether a decision you have made was a right or wrong one.

The tale of the Japanese farmer is instructive and illustrates how negative and positive circumstances co-exist and form a balance. What we perceive as right or wrong for us is not a gospel to live by. Any issue that requires us to take action to resolve it contains a possibility of wisdom or error of judgment. Individuals who want to take charge of their destiny must make decisions that risk either eventuality on a regular basis. We must endeavor to live with uncertain outcomes without letting them affect us.

An example of the above would be an employee who was fired. This might have been perceived as bad luck. He found a much better job almost immediately which would then seem like good luck. There are many examples of this balance all around us.

NOTES

YIN-YANG

Where there is Good there you will find Evil and where there is Right there will also be Wrong. In the Western way of thinking we persist with the erroneous belief that these concepts are mutually exclusive and antagonistic. We find it hard to reconcile how much they resemble each other and how they interact and evolve over time.

The concept of duality that exists in Eastern culture, simply put, is known as Yin-Yang. It does not refer exclusively to the opposition of good (Yin) with that of evil (Yang). It is also associated with the dual nature of reality itself and extends to physical and metaphysical states. So, we have light/dark, sound/silence, heat/cold, life/death, body/mind, movement/stillness and male/female for example. They are all indicative of the state of Yin-Yang. This evolving duality demonstrates that everything that occurs is complementary. For instance, the Yin of a cash-rich customer might have the Yang of a large, outstanding bill owing. Similarly, the Yang of a decline in sales might encourage the Yin of an innovatory product range to raise them again. As an advocate of Zen, Steve Jobs returned to a struggling company that had parted company with him after he had created it. We all know what happened to Apple after that.

By breaking down the graphical representation of Yin-Yang into its constituent parts we can see that each half incorporates a small circular component of the other. So within the soil of good there is a seed of evil and vice versa. The curved shape of each half also emphasizes how interdependent they are.

Sadly, in our Western state of ignorance and presumptuousness we assume that everything has an answer and that we can decide, in the moment, what will be the right one in every circumstance. We assume that the world turns as a consequence of our decision-making and we forget that, regardless of our input, "the sun rises, day after day".

As a symbol, the notion of Yin-Yang fits very well into our Western cultural environment and has become something of a cultural talisman. Many individuals new to Zen incorporate it into their sense of representational aesthetics. This might be in the form of a bracelet, pendant or Facebook icon to express a commitment to a lifestyle that focuses on maintaining harmony and balance with the environment. It is both a declaration of spiritual intent and a way to project a positive social image.

NOTES

KNOW YOURSELF

We have shared a fundamental concept with the East since the birth of our own culture and that is the overwhelming importance of knowing yourself. (Nosce te Ipsum)

To live according to your nature requires that you understand, and are aware, of what your nature truly is. This is by no means a simple task. The process of self-discovery, of knowing what fulfils you and what you feel, is in itself a definition of enlightenment in its purest sense. Men know intuitively that they enjoy football, beer and women even though the culture that they promote can appear sexist in some cases. It is down to the individual to separate honest interest in those pastimes and avoid some of the more misguided paths that might be followed instead. If only an advertising campaign could tap into the strong, emotional pull of these things and adapt it to products and services instead.

There are several ways to facilitate self-awareness, like introspective therapies for instance. The business world can offer the processes of self-evaluation, feedback and professional coaching. There is nothing as effective as total sincerity with yourself. Our outer persona can often become a constructed image that we project so that we appear more in control and professional. When we occupy positions of trust and authority or assume a supervisory role it is useful to hide our self-doubt and transmit confidence in ourselves and our abilities instead. At other times we have to pretend that we are confident even if we aren't. The reality is that we can attempt to live up to the image that other people have of us and promote the way we want to be perceived as much as we like. At night, in the darkness, we cannot hide from who we truly are and no one's opinion can help us when we only have a pillow for company.

To know ourselves is the first step to demonstrating true value in front of co-workers and associates whether they work with us or if they are third parties. Professional integrity should be understood as being a compromise between what one says and what one does. Honesty and integrity depends upon not confusing what you do by expressing a contradictory personal viewpoint at the same time. It is never wise to pretend to have expertise when you do not.

NOTES

BE TRUE TO YOURSELF

A Zen master, of many years, had been meditating with his student when he heard a noise in his garden pond. As he approached the pond he saw that a scorpion was struggling in the water and was sinking. The master held a twig out and tried to help the poor animal. The terrified scorpion reacted violently and tried to sting him. The monk pulled his hand away and watched the animal begin to struggle in the water once more. He tried to assist the scorpion again without hesitating. The Master's student was confused.

"But master, why do you try to save it? Can't you see that its nature is to attack?

The master replied to the student: "True, but my nature is to save it".

Your own nature exists in your heart and it determines how you feel towards your life and the things and people in it. If you take decisions that create a life that are contrary to what your heart instructs you to do then your conscious mind will be fighting a battle with itself that can never be won. Going against what you feel can only end in your own defeat.

Your actions should be tailored to your words. Your words should conform to your thoughts. Your thoughts should reflect the truth of your own nature. If you go against these simple rules then you can never hope to ignite the radiance that will enlighten you. Consequently, your path will be the wrong one.

Consider for a moment that you are at the top of a hierarchical relationship structure. Beneath you might be your children to be raised, your employees to be supervised or the members of a basketball team to be organized. The way each individual needs to be managed depends upon their individual personality and abilities. Some will need to be pampered and some will need clear and firm instructions. Some will need rewards and others will deserve penalties. Some can be left to their own devices whereas others will need strict discipline. If they act according to how they feel, as we should do ourselves, then we are required to adapt our own approach towards them as individuals. Your approach will reflect your own nature. If you are a taskmaster, you'll end up being hard on them. If you are docile, you'll end up being led by them. Those aspects of yourself that could be problematic when dealing with others should be finessed. Under no circumstances should you react to the people you lead.

NOTES

DO WHAT YOU REALLY LIKE

The path of Success depends on good hard work.

The amount of effort that you are prepared to put into your work -the long hours, thoroughness and personal sacrifice - will depend almost exclusively on the love you have for what you do. Work can be pure torture or a complete pleasure.

Zen teaches us that we can only excel at those things that we truly love. Only when we work from the perspective of love can we give ourselves up to a task with our body and our soul.

Alongside the acquisition of material wealth we can find a clear emotional component at work. To do what we love and achieve a goal is directly connected to that feeling of inner freedom that points directly towards the path of happiness.

This principle is directly applicable to all relationships whether they are personal or professional. This does not mean that we have to be unrealistic and assume that a regular eight hour day is a utopian ideal. It should be important enough to suit our nature and, as far as possible, be adapted to our personal needs. In most cases, an optimistic and positive approach towards work is representative of Zen. You should be able to find enough points of confirmation in your job to motivate you. This applies on a personal level as well. Approaching circumstances and relationships directly from a purely positive perspective allows us to find enough validation in them, both objectively and subjectively to progress enthusiastically and with an open heart. This is as true with violin lessons as it is with the state of matrimony.

It is essential to like the things we do because, otherwise, we would destroy our alarm clock every morning of our life.

This principle doesn't just apply to ourselves but is equally important in our dealings with other people. We are responsible for the motivation of the people around us as well. If we don't understand and utilize the knowledge of what they like to do then we can never guarantee our own success whether it is in the role of a leader, parent or organizer of the company party.

NOTES

KEEP BUSY

Zen teaches us that one of the best ways to distract ourselves from the workings of our conscious mind is to indulge in activities or hobbies. In this way we can use our mind and our body together to break the cycle of recurring concerns or worries that hold us back from reaching a state of Enlightenment.

In the Oriental culture the array of different activities is impressive and they are often influenced by antiquity. They range from archery, garden design, martial arts and caring for bonsai. One of the most influential aesthetic disciplines is the noble art of calligraphy. Currently Apple has popularized minimalism and defines what is *cool.*

Mentally relaxing and leisurely pastimes for Westerners can take a different form. We enjoy maintaining motorcycles, working in the garden or building Ikea flat-packed furniture. Even the ritual of applying make-up can assume a liberating meaning. Sport remains the most significant way of spending free time. Team-sports are very involving but it is as individuals that we derive the most satisfaction and detachment. When jogging in the park, the private mind acquires the purity of thought that we usually associate with a child. Unburdened from mundane concerns it can float from side to side and go from place to place like a butterfly in a garden that cannot settle in a single place. It is this weightlessness of mind where we find the greatest release and relaxation.

There are other liberating experiences as well. They can be group pastimes like having dinner with the girls at school or they can occur on a more personal level. A good novel -not a technical or business manual- can be the right choice and so can going to see a good movie. Sometimes a comedy can be more beneficial than a classic about art or literature. Even watching a TV game show could serve. In any event, it is preferable to playing Angry Birds even though it is the most successful App at the moment. You could even endure a trashy celebrity programme. The really liberating aspect of any activity is directly related to simply doing it. Sometimes it can hardly be called relaxation at all. That is better left to watching news reports, enjoying an interesting scientific documentary, film and little else.

NOTES

DISCONNECT

Within the ongoing process of releasing the mind, to create the circumstances in which we can be enlightened, we have seen that the objective is spontaneous illumination. To better facilitate this we must think without being conscious of thought. This requires us to focus our minds into a state of nothingness by freeing it first with a routine that obliges us to concentrate without settling on specific ideas.

Further to this, if it becomes necessary, we must have the ability to "reboot" our conscious mind as stated above. There are moments when it should be possible to accept that we are not on the right path, then retrace our steps, follow them back to the beginning and start from scratch. There are also times when our intuition tells us that we cannot continue a given course of action unless we detach ourselves from it by having a break. This could be in the form of a coffee, a snack or an afternoon off. It could also mean having a vacation or taking a sabbatical year. There are also instances when we must halt ourselves and bring everything to a stop around us. These moments of truth require that we demonstrate what we are really made of. We should accept that there are times when we must face ourselves and admit that we have to say NO.

A fundamental part of the process of disengagement is our understanding of how to say no. This is particularly true of a customer who expects us to give up our heart and soul to service their needs. It also applies to a project for which we have made insufficient preparation or a member of staff who is not only wasteful but who is unproductive and disruptive to his colleagues and us. It should be possible to say NO to a great idea that would consume too many resources. We must say NO to anything that would disturb the tranquility of mind essential for enlightenment.

The disconnection process must be integrated into our objective reality as well. It shouldn't be about taking a sabbatical year to pause and reflect on the importance of disconnecting and our ability to do so. A good example is a minor injury or case of the 'flu. We live our lives in a state of constant stress from top to bottom and we wrap ourselves in a web of obligations that prevent us from saying NO. We are like a broker working on Wall Street during the equivalent of another Black Thursday who sprains our ankle or develops a 39 degree fever. Thus forced to spend a few days at home we discover that nothing untoward happens in our absence as a result of us not servicing those obligations.

NOTES

ACT

Up to this point we have demonstrated a focused approach to Zen that coincides well with our collective understanding of it here in the West. We tend to associate it with meditation and such; with a purely mental state of being. We should not neglect that the reality we perceive via our senses is not there just to be interpreted by our mind. It is also created and affected by our actions. It becomes clear that action is instrumental in the process of enlightenment and gives it meaning.

We seek enlightenment to validate our actions because, otherwise, achieving it just for its own sake would be an empty resolution. So would the acquisition of knowledge as an end in itself. In the real world, the value of enlightenment, other than its intrinsic interest to us, rests in its application to action and the concrete results of that action taken.

In Zen, a single action means more than a thousand intentions. Only action has the power to transform its results into objective reality. In this way ideas are not as valuable as the concrete actions derived from them and, as such, the people who have ideas are not as significant as the ones with the capacity to translate ideas into quantifiable results. When a group of investors analyze a business plan they don't just scrutinize the plan itself or the possible returns that it might represent. They assess the capability of the individual making the pitch to carry the plan through as well. For this reason they are always predisposed to investing capital in businesses that are already established and have a track record of taking action. They would do this before taking risks on speculative plans that had never been actioned in any way.

There are always those individuals involved in projects both professional and personal who have a disturbing habit of using vague and speculative phrases when expressing their intentions. They will say "I will do this" or "I will improve that". In these cases it should be less important to visualize an ultimate goal than to take a first step that demonstrates a genuine desire to reach it. A well-worn phrase is "A long journey begins with a single step" but it remains one of the immutable truths of Zen. You can devote your mind to the benefits that meditation might bring you but it is only through the ability to put it into practice that those benefits can be appreciated.

NOTES

SIMPLIFY

In contrast to Zen, the human race has a natural tendency to take a simple thing and make it unnecessarily complicated. Therefore, by simplifying a process we are, in fact, getting closer to finding the purity that it possessed in its beginning. This ideal can apply to nature, people and ideas.

To succeed in this process of simplification, the reduction of the elements at stake within it is essential. We have already seen that we can help the workings of our mind if we occupy it with a single activity at a time instead of attempting to juggle a variety of simultaneous tasks. There is an example in Zen that perfectly illustrates this concept of simplicity in all things: the Zen garden. In it there are just a few elements. In general these comprise a small amount of bamboo, some sand and a small tower of stones that have been piled up. The peace that exists in the garden comes about as a result of the integration of these limited elements. Its tranquility would be compromised with the introduction of more numerous elements or concerns. Even the 3-4 pebbles in the archetypal Zen tower, increased to a dozen, would alter its perfect balance.

In this way, Pareto's Law fits perfectly with the notion that it's easier to balance and harmonize a subject with a few elements instead of many. This Italian economist stated that 20% of customers invariably generate 80% of the profits of a business. A good customer is not necessarily one who generates a lot of turnover. This intensive production process will come at the cost of resources consumed and the person-hours necessary to complete it. A good customer is, rather, one who provides you with a reasonable turnover that doesn't need the allocation of excessive resources. In the long-term, this type of customer will be better for the balance sheet.

On an individual level, an interesting exercise would comprise examining our own circumstances. These could include relationships and activities. We would then compare what these things provide us with against the resources they consume. It might become clear that we are squandering time, money and energy on things that provide us with very little. We could then simplify our life without compromising or denying ourselves anything.

NOTES

FOCUS

Within the continuing process of freeing up our mind, and simplifying the reality we find around us, we have discovered that concentrating on doing a single thing at any one time is essential. This is identifying the single point at issue or targeting.

This is a perfectly valid approach for the day to day situation and it is the way company directors function as well. It is vital both to comprehend that we must concentrate on the absolute essentials and also understand what essential really means in this context.

For companies, their strategic plan helps them define their objective, vision and values.

It is more complicated in the case of individuals.

One way would be to dedicate a minute, but no more, to remember someone who is no longer with us and then speculate as to what that person might be doing now if they were alive. Then, imagine what the same situation would be in your own case. Consider the things that you will lose and the people who would no longer be with you. Imagine what it would be like without them.

Okay, done? Whatever you thought of in this moment is precisely what you should be focusing on in your life now. The notions you had are those things that mean the most to you and the people you brought to mind are the ones that really mean something. The sum of these two components is what makes you happy and what you should be focusing on. It is possible that the majority of those people are within easy reach but if they aren't and you really need them you should go for it. You should look for ways to display this importance permanently. This might be via writing or looking for a picture that evokes memories. Place it at the top of your priority list, use it as wallpaper for your computer and use a post-it to display it everywhere. Don't be afraid to let everyone know what it means. A public commitment to do a certain thing is often the greatest stimulus towards achieving that end.

NOTES

IF YOU FALL, GET BACK UP

"In a time of failure you will find the best season to plant the seeds of success."

Yogananda

The path of Zen tells us that if you fall seven times then you will get up eight times. Every time you rise to your feet you will do so with less fear than before, with more experience and strength.

Think for a moment. How many failures have been experienced by your company? A disastrous campaign, that disloyal employee or the miracle product that nobody wanted to buy. I'm sure that you will know of many examples with just as many projects that hit the mark.

Think for a moment about the consequences of those failures. Was anyone injured? Was any irreparable damage caused? Did the company cease trading?

Even on a personal level, despite the fact that feelings again play a decisive role, we can see how the passage of time makes everything relative and finesses the extent of the disappointments. All of those pumpkins that were given to us at the end of year dance just become simple anecdotes.

The path of Zen teaches us how to integrate the failures as being a natural part of the learning process towards enlightenment. In this way there is no greater failure than that which has convinced us that we cannot succeed. This is the failure of not trying. Without pushing out too far into space and time you will find that most elderly people will admit the same thing. They regret those things that they haven't done more than things they have done.

There is another precept in Zen that encourages us to get to our feet after a setback. It tells us that failure is in the past not in the now. Stand with your back facing the road you have already traveled on and face the way ahead it recommends. Any failure was the result of an action already taken so it is nothing that can be changed. It needs to be forgotten.

Failure is, in any case, a detour on the road and not a dead-end street (Zig Ziglar). The important thing is to get up as soon as possible and get back on track without losing too much time on licking our wounds. They will heal themselves in time.

NOTES

LEAVE YOUR MARK

Through enlightenment, we understand our commitment to the world and the transcendence of our actions within it. There is a somewhat philosophical concept of Zen which establishes the absence of the ego to the extent that the "I" only exists in relation to everything that surrounds us. We are the “not I” because “I” can exist anywhere: in a plant, in a stream. In short we must value this, because we believe it and that's all. I understand and I share the belief that this formulation of the concept may be seen as ordure and, as such, is likely to generate some skepticism.

However, there is in nature, a very important concept. It states that there is nothing more significant than the consciousness of belonging to something greater than ourselves. In turn, this encourages a sense of belonging, responsibility and fuller awareness of the importance of our actions. When a dental surgeon performs surgery on a patient to insert a titanium implant, he can choose to be believe that it is merely "putting a few screws into a client" or on the contrary that he “is improving the oral health of a patient". Perhaps the difference is not very clear at the professional level, but from the perspective of personal commitment there is a gulf.

The translation of this is the willingness to participate in a certain concept of common good (shared in part with other religions). This participation results in a certain sensitivity towards solidarity, transparency, gratitude and everything that is considered politically correct in general, integrating concepts that are traditionally included within the Corporate Social Responsibility strategy of companies such as environmental policies, life-work balance or non-discrimination programs.

Therefore, we must not renounce the purity of Values (in capitals). If you dress up a bad product in order to sell it, perhaps you will succeed in the short term. However, but only a long-term vision will lead us to enjoy the strength of the balance compared to the volatility of short term success. Therefore, companies that rely solely on their prices may be fleeting. Those who rely on their products will survive the abyss of obsolescence. But those who rest on their Values, will be eternal thanks to loyal customers and consolidated products.

NOTES

POSITIVE ENERGY

A traveler came to a village and asked a Zen Master: "What are the people of this town like?"
"What do you think? The Master replied.
"They seem like they're good people" the traveler observed
"Yes, that is quite right" the Master agreed. Soon a second traveler arrived and asked the same question as the first.
"What are the people in this town like?"
"What do you think?" the Master said once more.
"They seem evil" the traveler observed.
"Yes, that is quite true" agreed the master.
The student who was with the Master expressed his surprise:
"Master" he asked "why did you agree with them when they said different things?"
"I did no such thing" the Master stated "we always find what we expect"

Optimism is the foundation upon which the actions we take are supported. Optimism is what determines the positivity or negativity of the inner strength of our actions. It tilts the balance toward either Yin or Yang.

If we have a negative initial attitude like mistrust, for example, our own actions reveal it. However subtle these indications might be, either a glance or a word, they can still tip the balance towards negativity in a potentially devastating manner. Whereas, a positive attitude, if you trust someone for instance, has the opposite effect. Although equally subtle, a smile or a warm greeting immediately tilts the balance towards the positive. The difference between a vicious circle and a virtuous circle can be found in a soft initial push which unleashes a series of subsequent actions and associated reactions. This is often how we define the future.

In any case, it is our responsibility to introduce positivity in our lives. Even though we cannot control the events that happen to us we can, nevertheless, regulate our reactions to them. For instance, if a car makes an improper maneuver we can put it out of our mind immediately or we can sound our horn over and over again, wind down the window and swear loudly. Neither of our reactions will alter the maneuver but they will affect our well-being in different ways. The former will break our attachment to the event in a few seconds but the latter will make you remember it all day and relive your anger continually.

NOTES

THE EGO

The path of Zen tells us that the Ego can be our greatest enemy but it can also become our greatest ally.

An excess of ego prevents us from having sufficient humility to properly pursue the path of Zen. Without accepting and acknowledging our shortcomings, our weaknesses and our fears, any kind of personal evolution to a higher level will be impossible. The greatest danger represented by the ego is that it separates the individual from all that surrounds him. This undermines the concept of harmonious integration with our environment, and can affect our personal or professional relationships, our place in society and even in the world itself. In fact, pure Zen advocates, in a radical way, the utter renunciation of the Ego as an essential pre-requisite to achieving Enlightenment.

However, our Ego also defines our identity, our character and our nature. This last point is fundamental in achieving a harmonious relationship with the people around us. We must be aware of ourselves as individuals. We must have confidence in who we are and where we intend to go. Ego allows us to do these things with self assuredness so that the people around us can perceive it.

The Ego is like a horse. If it is calm and docile it will not take you very far. If it is powerful and wild you will need to break it and train it not to harm you. If you can learn to control it though, it will take you very far.

The Zen principle of harmony between your nature and the reality around you is easier to achieve if you develop an honest way to transmit your nature to the people around you in a sincere way. To achieve this you must have your own voice and let it be heard. This should be done with respect and with self-confidence. It is only by being assertive that you can achieve a harmonious relationship with the people around you. To achieve this, you should be able to speak clearly with a direct message which is easy to understand. It doesn't matter about the beauty of the words. It is more about the effectiveness of communicating the idea you wish to transmit. A clear, reassuring, message encourages security, a friendly word provides optimism and a calming sentence earns trust. All of these things, when placed together, provide leadership.

NOTES

ZEN IS BALANCE

The fundamental principle of Zen is the balance that is achieved through harmony between your mind and your environment. It is easier to harmonize a few items rather than many items. Therefore, one of the characteristic features of Zen is the simplicity of forms and concepts, purity without artifacts, as seen in the classical representation of a Zen garden.

But above all, the Balance described must be an inner balance: the balance has to be *inside* you. You must take care of it. This may seem like a very individualistic approach, but the fact is that Zen focuses greatly on the well-being of the individual - for this reason it provides so much inner peace. Nevertheless, it knows that harmony with the environment is in the best interests of the individual. For this reason, it is concerned about the balance of everything that surrounds us, be it our job, our families, our hobbies, our mind, our spirituality, our body, or even our role on the Parent Teacher Committee.

In order to obtain a balance with the environment, we should not forget that we will only reach optimum balance if we are at peace with our own nature, whatever it may be. . It is not that Zen is amoral or does not value ethics, it is clear that honest and ethical behavior helps to maintain balance with our environment, resulting in harmony, inner peace ... but in reality Zen only has truth and self-awareness. It does not aim to tell you what to do but it will give you the mechanisms to decide for yourself and be at peace with your decisions. It's not about the "goodness" of it. If someone offends you, it won't tell you to turn the other cheek, instead it will try to help you to decide if you should walk away or react with violence. It is clear that an aggressive reaction will most probably produce imbalance and will steer us from the path. But only you can make that decision.

All in all, what is important is that you feel comfortable with yourself and your decisions. Think of the typical image of Buddha (the first man who reached enlightenment). We see a plump man who is smiling and relaxed. Does he look stressed out? Definitely not. To me he seems like someone who is happy not with the life he has been given, but the one he has chosen to live in harmony and balance with everything around him.

NOTES

ZEN AMBITION

Despite the role of simplification to achieve balance, we can not reach fullness unless we have a healthy ambition to pursue all the good things life has to offer. For example, we should aim to evolve and improve, and to strive to achieve our dreams.

In any case, this ambition doesn't have to be incompatible with the fundamental concepts of Zen: renunciation. This doesn't mean the renunciation associated with many Western religions, but instead it should be understood as a process of acceptance of failures. We should value them as a learning resource. In fact, Zen searches for evolution, a constant improvement of personal development which is perfectly compatible with our personal ambition. It must be an ambition that is honest, realistic, and that does not cause us stress, anxiety or frustration. We should pursue achievable goals that allow us to enjoy the journey. For this, it is only necessary to say no to those things that demand more of us than what they give us back in return. Also, anything that doesn't correspond with our personal dreams that are born from our own nature and that will make us happier. In this sense, buying a Ferrari may satisfy our Ego and our social status compared to that of our neighbors. Satisfying our inquisitiveness about driving a sports car could put us in a good mood for a few days, but will it really make us happier in absolute terms?

Thanks to the integration of the concept of renunciation provided by Zen, Western ambition becomes a motivating and inspiring ambition. We can never have everything that we wish for. In fact, reaching inner peace doesn't depend so much on absolute goals. It is about enjoying the journey as well as our achievements along the way. We don't need to be able to run like an olympic athlete to be fit. Neither do we have to be millionaires to have a good relationship with money.

However, this ambition is (and should remain) the driving force that helps us move forward: Eastern culture itself has many examples that invite improvement: from the caste system of Hinduism to continuous improvement in Kaizen.

NOTES

METHODOLOGY

ZEN GUIDE

The principles of the Zen Revolution that appear in this book are followed by a large number of people thanks to the Zen Guide on RevolucionZen.com

The majority of people only need a month or so to start enjoying the benefits of the Zen Revolution. Many of them still depend upon the support of a wide range of useful recommendations and specific steps that are proposed by the website.

As we have seen, if we move forward on the path of Zen it's relatively simple. It can be very useful to find some form of confirmation to remind us that we are on the right path and to assist us on our long journey to inner peace with concrete and specific actions instead of thoughtful reflections.

In this sense, perhaps the actions that are the most valued by users of RevolucionZen.com are those which focus on positive thinking. Think of something good that has happened today, or a person who has been a positive influence on you. Equally, the other exercises that are most valued are the positive messages that the Web allows you to forward to your friends. The guidelines that try to reduce, albeit only modestly, our dependence on the mobile phone are also popular. There are also exercises to "step back from things" that are regularly suggested and popular. If the ultimate goal is to be able to distance ourselves from anything that causes stress or concern we should begin with exercises that are straightforward. They encourage modest, easy to introduce, disconnections in our daily routine. Using the example of the mobile phone, we could put it on silent when we eat. If we are obliged to do it in the cinema, why not at home? Perhaps the most popular activities are those that promote playfulness. In fact, the custom of fortune cookies is followed not only by the individuals who enjoy it in the moment, but also by friends who share it with contacts on social networks.

In any event they are specific actions and measures. The experience shows that the typical book containing 500 philosophical quotes will only overload you. Therefore, the Zen revolution is simply more effective. You suggest only five quotes and it invites you to think and reflect on them for a couple of minutes. In Zen, as in life, its better to set yourself ask a few realistic objectives rather than attempt to make big changes to your life overnight.

Perhaps the most surprising thing about the Zen Revolution is the amount of people who simply give this book as a gift or recommend it to others. It could be this book or the “Zen space” with the exercises that appear on the website. What better gift can there be than giving a tool with which anyone can access their inner peace and live a better life with less stress? In fact, there are some companies that have already started to offer some of their customers, or VIP members, peace of mind. Bearing this in mind, there is an interesting example of a hotel chain that has a copy of this book placed in every room to demonstrate its commitment to its customers and to their peace of mind.

And on the topic of companies, more and more managers consider Revolution Zen to be an easy way to somehow help their employees.

Maybe some of these executives will do so simply because they have realized the medium term benefits with relation to profits. Some do so, simply to be politically correct within a CSR strategy. However, the vast majority do so because they have understood (and have gladly accepted) their responsibility to obtain a Zen balance in the company. It will no doubt dilute negativity, apathy and "bad vibes" and open the door to renewed optimism, teamwork and contagious energy. It is as though an "epidemic of proactivity" has been unleashed.

Furthermore, the testimonies of many of these managers note that thanks to Revolution Zen, there has been a certain awakening in the spirituality of the Company. Values can (and should) become one of the main assets of a company. It is undeniable that the companies that rely strongly on their values can cope better with the economic crisis. However, is one of the most difficult assets to manage: communicating those values can be relatively simple, but whether employees take them on board or not is a truly utopian task. Thanks to the stimulus of Zen Revolution, discussing topics such as respect for clients, commitment to environmental issues and sustainability, or the commitment to quality, has never been easier. Not only are these concerns a natural part of the director's speech, but they are also integrated within a common project in which everyone is aware of their commitment to contribute their part.

In any case, it is also interesting to note that they all agree with the ease of implementation and highlight the good reception from the staff that has willfully embraced the initiative.

Perhaps the most important element of Zen Guide (and the proposed method) is the total absence of obligations. It's amazing to see how people are in a rush to get away from work at midday, eating junk food in a stressful manner in the car while driving to a yoga class with the objective of “relaxing”. After the class, they then go back to work stressed out yet again, because they are going to be late for a meeting.

It is certainly much better to simply aim for a minimal scenario for relaxation. Each person can do so according to their circumstances (time, family, work, ...). A place where, once inside it you can find a neutral atmosphere where it is possible to make simple steps in avoiding all types of artificial influences.

Therefore, for the Zen Revolution you can remove tunics, incense and the tinkling of bells completely out of the equation. You can focus only on the depth, because only there can you find the answers that allow you to be who you really are.

ZEN MOMENTS

Life can be full of those special moments that connect our inner self with the reality of the world that surrounds us. These are the moments when we can really be ourselves and feel that we are truly alive:

- When we are able to relax with the morning coffee and, perhaps, read the newspaper.
- Leaving the gym after a workout, freshly showered.
- Enjoying a siesta in the summer.
- Looking into a crackling fireplace.
- Feeling the respiration of a baby while it sleeps in our arms.
- Spending a whole afternoon watching football with our friends or just going shopping with them.
- The sensation we feel in our skin when we wash our hands with warm water and a surplus of slippery soap.
- Walking outside after a rainstorm when we can smell the wet earth all around us.
- Feeling the sand under our bare feet when walking along a beach in springtime.

- Driving along a deserted road as a light, autumn rain falls.

It is important to be aware of the fullness of those moments and how they influence our way to the path of inner peace. They can assist us, through their combination of balance and harmony, to progress along the path to enlightenment through Zen.

Although we have seen that there can be sublime moments to be found spending time in the company of others, Zen moments are, by contrast, mainly moments of relaxation and intimacy with ourselves alone. Although our society tends towards underestimating the value of solitude, from the Zen perspective it is not only desirable but necessary. After all, we ourselves are the best friend that we will ever have, or want, and we know that it is a friend who will never leave us. Every moment spent alone is merely an opportunity to be accompanied by ourselves. It is certain that every busy mother knows, beyond doubt, how precious those moments are that they can spend dedicated only to themselves. This is, in itself, a time of Zen.

In short, the importance of Zen lies ultimately in our increasing awareness of the transcendence of these moments. We need to realize the extent to which they help us concentrate fully on the Here and Now. In those moments, at its precise instant, we are no longer parents or mothers. We are not employees or teachers. Neither are we doctors, neighbors or friends. We are just ourselves and, as such, we do not owe anything to anyone. Nothing should disturb us or bother us and we must lose all awareness of any kind of restrictions. We feel free, at peace with ourselves and with our environment. We are then able to relax and let ourselves go.

In light of this, the Zen Revolution suggests and invites everyone to publish their own Zen moment on the website or via their Facebook page o Twitter account. Perhaps others, reading the explanation of your moment, will become sufficiently inspired by it to become more aware of their own. They might seek their moments out for themselves.

ZEN ATTITUDE

We have seen that the Zen Guide is a set of activities to help us focus on Zen. However, the Zen Revolution doesn't aim to provide strict guidelines, but instead it shows us a type of Zen that each person can adapt to their own realities.

It is clear that the attitude of the individual is vital for the Zen approach to be successful. Zen tells us to meet it with the "mind of a child". This means embracing it with curiosity and accepting it without prejudice while assuming that there are always infinite possibilities. In this way our attitude should be open, positive, trusting, and, most importantly, consistent. It is not about obsessing ourselves with getting on with the path more quickly. Nothing could be further from the truth. Yet, at all times be aware that there is a path and each of us made the decision to go along it at our own pace. We do this without pressures of any kind but always with the utmost determination.

Simply put, any religion, take Christianity for example, is based on three guiding principles. Those are faith, practice and commitment. In the case of the Western style of Zen demonstrated here-which at no time professes to be a religious doctrine-these principles are relative.

- With reference to faith, Zen only requires us to have belief in ourselves and not necessarily in a higher being. This question relates more to the personal belief of each individual.

- With reference to practice you must first look for flexibility and comfort. It is more of an *à la carte* practice to the extent that the decision to follow the path of Zen is a free one. Each individual, depending on their circumstances, wishes and concerns can determine their own degree of involvement where the level of practice proposed by Zen is concerned. As it is not a religion, there are no formal ceremonies or sacred rituals to be followed. There are, instead, some modest exercises that help us to reflect on the path. It is a path that we follow at our own pace. It is one that we have decided to walk of our own free will.

- Lastly, the question of commitment itself is crucial to the path of Zen. Naturally, as in other issues of Zen Revolution, there is no kind of obligation in respect of it. Even when we are serious in our intent, it is very difficult to obtain a result if we are not fully committed.

Therefore, your commitment becomes the defining principle of the Zen attitude. To demonstrate that our devotion is sincere and true we must, most importantly, carry it with us whilst also displaying it for the benefit of third parties as well. Public displays of our belief can take the form of wallpaper motifs, a photo that might accompany a comment on Facebook, an inspiring retweet, replacing your profile image to that of Buddha, the Yin Yang worn on a necklace or t-shirt and even mentioning Zen to your friends or pinning its message onto a bulletin board.

The advantage of displaying your Zen attitude publicly is that on the one hand it increases your level of commitment in front of third parties. It also facilitates and enhances the quality of your relationships: when you see someone using Zen symbols, you know that they have a positive attitude, that they are conciliatory, consistent and can be a good influence That person will also see the same in you.

In short, to recap the basics of the Zen movement is to know that with your good example in front of others you are always giving out a message of harmony and balance. This is not just good news for your own image. It is also auspicious for your future prospects. Basically, life always hands us the fruits of the seeds that we have already sown.

TEST

As in any path that one should follow, it is important to realize where it begins before we can understand the significance of the path, our eventual destination and what we might expect to discover as we go along it.

For this it is fundamental to know today what our initial level of Zen is, how balanced our life is, the degree of harmony that we have with our surroundings and the people around us and the alignment of our reality with our true nature.

The Zen Revolution offers two simple tests to help us measure our degree of Zen. The first Test is focused strictly upon the individual or personal level. The second is more focused on the professional field and it concentrates more on the reality of business or employment.

The only requirement for its elaboration is the absolute understanding of who we really are and not who we would like to be. In both cases, the analysis of the results that we obtain should help us to realize our true selves and reflect on where we want to take our life or our company in the future. It might be a cliché but today really is the first day of the rest of your life. Consider whether the answer you give today will be the same as the answer that you will give if the question is asked again in five years time. If the answer is no you must realize that it is your decision and only you can decide to begin making the small steps in that direction.

Zen Test
PERSONAL

5= Always
4= Often
3= Sometimes
2= Rarely
1= Never

[ ] Do you make your own decisions?
You do what you want, not what others expect of you.
[ ] Are you looking for the answers within yourself?
You assume that you are ultimately responsible for yourself.
[ ] Do you accept that there are things that lie beyond your reach?
You can't always control everything nor should you try to.
[ ] Do you think things are relative?
Good things are not THAT good and bad things are never so serious.
[ ] Do you know how to concentrate on the present?
It's not worth thinking too much about the things that have happened in the past or over-thinking what might happen in the future.
[ ] Do you act responsibly?
You are aware of the results of your actions.
[ ] Do you have confidence in the future, yourself and other people?
You are optimistic that everything will be okay
[ ] Do you accept who you are?
You feel comfortable with your life and yourself generally.
[ ] Do you have good personal habits?
Food, health, exercise, rest
[ ] Do you trust yourself?
You have trust in your instincts and your abilities
[ ] Do you feel a real sense of satisfaction when you achieve your goals?
You enjoy the moment. You do not need to think about the next goal
[ ] Do you have good relationships with the people around you?
Family, friends, colleagues.
[ ] Are you good at managing stress?
You avoid complications, you find solutions and maintain distance
[ ] Do you care what others think of you? *
You should know your own opinion and strive to be positive
[ ] Is something missing in your life? *
You feel that you can improve some things in your life

[ ] TOTAL Score

Your Zen level is:

Over 60: Excellent
BETWEEN 51 AND 60: Above Average
BETWEEN 41 AND 50: Average
BETWEEN 31 AND 40: Below Average
BELOW 30: Poor

** The questions marked with an asterisk may have ambiguous results:*

- *Concern about what others think of you may indicate an ego that is too pronounced. It might also suggest a sense of belonging to an environment and a willingness to interact in harmony with it.*

- *The sensation that something is missing from your life may indicate a void but also an awareness of an absence which is a motivation to try to work to fill it.*

Zen Test
BUSINESS

5= Always
4= Often
3= Sometimes
2= Rarely
1= Never

[ ] Do all the staff has a clear understanding of the business strategy?
It is well defined and transmitted about what the company is involved in, its fundamentals, its intentions, its value system and where it sees itself in the future.

[ ] The specific objectives are clear and in line with the strategy?
What you are required to do is clearly defined and consistent with the outlined strategy.

[ ] Do they devote sufficient resources to achieving them? *Once a goal is defined it is assigned the resources necessary for achieving it in regards to time, personnel and training*

[ ] Is there real leadership from management?
Staff perceives that the management is in good hands and they feel confident in the decisions that are made by them.

[ ] Is the employer-employee relationship free from serious labor disputes?
The relationship and communication between staff and management remains smooth.

[ ] Is the staff sufficiently motivated?
There are proactive mechanisms in place to encourage feedback and contributions from staff. These comprise: recognition in public and private, delegating tasks, projection, compensation, flexibility, transparency and the encouragement of creativity and innovation in the workplace. This runs counter to the negative stimuli of pressure, recrimination, threats and punishment.

[ ] Is there a good atmosphere among the staff?
The circumstances favor a good working environment among employees: without arguments, favoritism or discrimination of any kind.

[ ] Do you encourage Corporate Social Responsibility?
There is an ongoing concern for quality, awareness of responsibility towards third parties such as customers, staff, suppliers and society in general. There are, in addition, active environmental policies and corporate conscience.

[ ] Is there long-term vision?
The business operates from the perspective of not only short-term economic performance but also the strength and sustainability of the company in the future.

[ ] Does the company have a work environment that is free of stress? *There is a relaxed working environment that applies regardless of the level of productivity.*

[ ] TOTAL Score

The level of Zen in Business is:

Over 60: Excellent
BETWEEN 51 AND 60: Above Average
BETWEEN 41 AND 50: Average
BETWEEN 31 AND 40: Below Average
BELOW 30: Poor

EPILOGUE

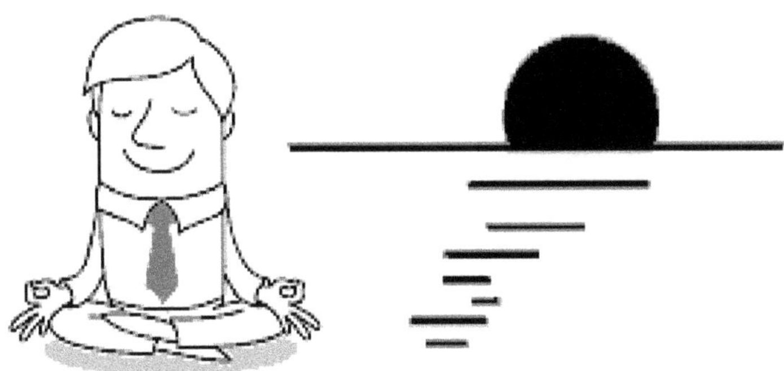

As you have seen, Zen aims to create the personal conditions, especially the mental ones, so you can move forward with confidence towards a destiny that you forge yourself with your own decisions. The process that enables you to see clearly which decisions will make you feel more content with your true nature is known as "enlightenment" or "realization" as the Buddhists are used to characterizing it. However, it is not really a tangible goal but more like an attitude towards life that is perfectly compatible with the daily routine of our Western reality. Despite its Eastern origin, the integration of a Zen philosophy that is adapted to our culture is relatively simple. Indeed, the values that underpin it have been present in our own society for a long time.

The Zen masters who have read the Bible all agree that Jesus Christ was an enlightened individual. They can acknowledge when someone has seen the truth whether or not they can agree on it between themselves. While other religions oblige us to believe in a god, Zen simply suggests that we believe in something much closer and that is ourselves. Equally, the concept of a life everlasting which is inherent in other religions doesn't fit in with the realistic or pragmatic viewpoint of Zen. Zen prefers to seek the reward in this life not in the next one. Despite this, Zen does not present a religious problem because it only asks one thing of you: to have faith in yourself.

Nevertheless, this "compatibility" between Zen and religion, in its role as the fundamental philosophical axis of the development of Western culture, isn't just apparent. It permeates through the entire spectrum of Western society.

John Lennon with his song "Imagine" can be taken as a clear example. Perhaps an even better representative would be Steve Jobs, one of the corporate icons of our time. His untimely death emphasized his significance even more profoundly. He has become a benchmark by being a visionary who, with courage and perseverance, managed to make Apple not merely a corporate paradigm but, through it, came to influence society like few people in business had ever done before. Simply put, he was able to see things differently.

Zen was a consistent and clear influence on the life of Steve Jobs. In fact, his famous speech at the graduation ceremony at Stanford University in 2005, in which he advanced his theory of "join the dots" and which concluded with the mythical "stay hungry, stay foolish" quote is vital to understanding the summary of his philosophy. For Jobs, the influence of Zen began in the early 70's. It was an inspiration to him throughout his life and his business career.

The list of personalities who we, in one way or another, might consider enlightened within our cultural environment may be quite large, but it is perhaps more important that each one of us looks at examples that are closer to our reality. Then we can find our own inspirational figures. People who have advanced enough along the path of Zen, even though they might be unaware of it, emit an invaluable, inspirational light. You should not fail to follow any light that you discover on your way. This could take the form of reading this book on the ascent of a mountain, at a meeting with friends or at a colleague's farewell dinner.

With reference to this book, if you believe that you have reached a state of enlightenment by reading it, or even by getting to the end of it, it will be because you haven't quite understood its true meaning. If you think about it I have, at no time, attempted to explain in detail or in a systematic way what Zen actually is. I have simply focused on the concepts and tools that will enable you to intuit that within these pages there is an indefinable “something”, whatever Zen is, that can be useful in your life. Perhaps you saw a glimmer of inspiration during your reading and it helped you to define a pattern to take you forward. You will find more help to achieve this if you visit RevolutionZen.com and try the Zen exercises there. In the appendix to this book you'll find some examples of these. Be aware, however, that true enlightenment can only be found if you follow the path of Zen yourself.

Nevertheless, if you have reached this point then the seed of Zen is already inside you. In time it will begin to germinate until it blossoms. For some it will remain a soft, warm glow, for others it will become a blazing lighthouse. In any case, the important thing is that the radiance never goes out. If you ever need it, you know that you will find it again if you look inside yourself because it is there within you. It always has been. At heart, in this book I have not proposed anything that was not already within you, nothing that you didn't already know and nothing that you haven't already been pursuing forever. It is something about which you've never stopped asking questions.

However, despite the answers that have been arrived at so far, you should not assume that the search is over because, in reality, it has merely begun.

In truth, the search begins today, here and now. .

Welcome to Zen.

NOTES

EXERCISES

The next exercises are a small sample of those available on our website.

www.ZenRevolution.com

EXERCISES

- You should try to do these exercises at the same time, in the same place, and under the same circumstances. Therefore, it is up to each one to determine whether this dynamic is compatible with their weekend routine or if it is limited to the working week.

- You should try – where possible – to do them in a relatively calm and neutral place, but it doesn't have to be a *sanctuary.*

- You only need to dedicate 5 minutes a day, except in exceptional cases

- It is interesting to reflect and analyze the exercises, but you can be very brief with your answers. It's not about writing, but more about getting used to thinking with a Zen focus. Being made to write helps us to focus our thoughts.

- Nevertheless, after each exercise, it is useful to keep in mind the lessons of the exercise in question for some time afterwards and analyze the possible implications on our own particular situations.

- Do not start more than one exercise per day. It is important thing to internalize them fully. For this, we must allow for enough time between exercises.

- If one day you are unable to "follow" the Guidelines don't worry. You can carry on the next day.

Exercise 1.

Date _ _ / _ _ / _ _

Describe something positive that has happened this week. It doesn't have to be something exceptional or unique; it could be simple everyday fact.

Thinking of positive things is essential in order to stay positive, calm and relaxed. This is what is known as "Positive Thinking".

Through daily practice (of which we will perform several variations), we can train our mind to focus on identifying positive things we usually overlook. Equally, we will be more aware of just how many positive things there are in our lives, and how privileged we are, as well as the influence of our actions in a positive spiral.

Exercise 2.

Date _ _ / _ _ / _ _

You are a basketball coach (or any other sport) and your team is losing at half-time.

Before you start the second part, you must be able to motivate your players. You may not tell them off for their mistakes during the first half, as it no longer forms part of the "Now". Instead, you should encourage them by transmitting your confidence in them with positive messages. You must be able to visualize the changing rooms and *feel* the steam from the showers, hear the shouts of the players as they regain faith in themselves, the roar of the public when they go back on court ready to conquer the world. Think of a sentence from that speech.

Think of motivating facts that help maintain their high level of self-confidence, self-esteem and optimism. Also, this helps them to be aware of our own ability to motivate ourselves, which in turn increases our autonomy and sense of responsibility to ourselves.

Exercise 3.

Date __/__/__

Think about someone - or something - that really annoys you.

Now, imagine that a company has employed you, for an impressive salary, to advocate the very thing, or the individual, that you dislike so much.

As “counsel for the defense” you must present arguments in favor of someone who pays your salary but whose position never coincides with yours.

Most conflicts arise from someone's opposition to a fixed position we adopt that we usually base on our own preconceived ideas. If we used our imagination to view ourselves from another individual's point of view we would better appreciate how much easier it would be to establish and maintain a more harmonious balance with the environment around us. It is through this approach of empathy that we discover that there are no extremes like black or white. There is merely a multiplicity of things that are tinted by shades of grey. Everyone has a valid viewpoint seen from their own position even though they may annoy us sometimes.

Exercise 4.

Date _ _ / _ _ / _ _

Think carefully about something that went wrong in the past - something that you can laugh about now.

Describe very briefly what happened, how you felt at that time and how you feel about it now.

Although there may always be scars that never heal, in the vast majority of cases "time heals everything", so we do not have a reason for uneasiness, fear or distress.

Even if our irrational fears are met, "tomorrow morning the sun will still rise", and eventually we will see that we end up accepting it, getting over it or simply forgetting it. Nevertheless, in times of trouble we tend to forget this reality. It is therefore advisable to accustom our minds to realizing exercises of acceptance and self-improvement like these; if we do so, we will be able to cope with occasional setbacks in our lives.

Exercise 5.

Date _ _ / _ _ / _ _

If we want life to be good to us, we have to be good with it and everything that surrounds us. This means that we have the obligation to do good things. The best way to fulfill that obligation is to help people, and to do so every day of our lives. This does not mean you have to perform heroic acts, instead it could mean small gestures of kindness like helping a friend fix their computer or listening to a friend who is going through a rough patch.

Is there something you could do in your day to provide something good for someone?

There are many proverbs in all languages that describe the relationship between what we contribute to life and what we get from it.

Take note of it and ask yourself each night if we have done well to others or if we have helped someone. This is the best way to remember the importance of fulfilling our obligation to do good.

THANKS

First, I would like to thank Bernard Royal (Senzuto Tchen) for his inspiring advice. Bernard was the Director of Systems Development in Paris during a dark period a few years ago due to a wave of suicides of the employees of French companies in the telecommunications sector. Unlike many of his colleagues, Bernard decided to take action and move forward by embracing Zen with the same passion and methodology he uses when designing technological solutions. After a long time in Tibet, Bernard has managed the difficult balance of internalizing Zen without losing his own Western roots, as well as the prodigious ability to merge two well known concepts in the Business world. Your input has been instrumental in reviving the passion for Zen in me 20 years after I initially discovered it at UCSD (University of California - San Diego), during which time my motivation was diluted as I saw the difficulty of applying Mondos, Koans, Zazens and Sesshins to the

daily reality of the Western world, as well as its lack of practical value in both private life and especially in the Business world.

I would also like to thank the teachers and Makori Tzu Tzu and Mikon Kensho their contributions and corrections on the purest aspects of Eastern culture and philosophy. I thank them for their tolerance of my eclectic approach towards Zen. They feel so much love for humanity and are so confident about what Zen can bring to people. They who have not hesitated to support me regardless of the fact that the purity of Zen they practice has been relativized by a more pragmatic approach.

Thanks also to the entire team Ingética, led by my partner Jaume González, for the excellent technology used in designing the on-line exercises that complete the reading of this book.

Also, my thanks to Annie McGinnis for her editorial dedication and all the people who have made the publication of my books possible: Maureen Williams, Katty Jones, David Koxet, Andrew Gunner, Jenny Jonas and, especially, Robert Belenguer: capacity analysis is exhausting and inspiring at the same time, thank you.

Naturally, thanks to each and every one of the readers and subscribers on zenrevolution.com (and revolucionzen.com) for their contributions, comments and suggestions. But mostly for the strength of their presence and their encouraging words of thanks: you have seen that helping someone is the most powerful motivation to carry on giving everything.

And finally, thanks to my family. My parents for showing the value of unconditional support, my wife for helping me get through each day without exception, and with the sacred obligation to laugh. Finally thanks to my children for being the very essence of Zen.

REFERENCES

- David Pollack, Zen Poems of the Five Mountains, 1985.
- Eugen Herrigel, Zen in the Art of Archery. New York: Vintage Books, 1971.
- Stephanie Wada, The Oxherder: A Zen Parable Illustrated. NY: George Braziller, 2002.
- Robert A.F. Thurman, trans., The Holy Teaching of Vimalakirti, 1976.
- Frederic Spiegelberg, Zen, Rocks & Waters. NY: Pantheon, 1961.
- Carl Bielefeldt, Dogen's Manuals of Zen Meditation, 1988.
- Lu K'uan Yü, Ch'an and Zen Teaching (2 series), 1960.
- Giei Sato and Eshin Nishimura, Unsui: A Diary of Zen Monastic Life
- Richard Hughes Seager, Buddhism in America. NY: Columbia University Press, 1999.
- Paul Wienpahl, The Matter of Zen. London: George Allen & Unwin, 1965.
- Philip Kapleau, The Three Pillars of Zen, rev. ed., 1980.
- Shin'ichi Hisamatsu, Zen and the Fine Arts. Tokyo: Kodansha International, 1971.
- Robert Aitken, Taking the Path of Zen. San Francisco: North Point Press, 1982.
- Nan Shin (Nancy Amphoux). Diary of a Zen Nun. London: Rider & Co., 1987.
- Thich Nhat Hanh, Zen Keys, 1974.
- John Daido Loori, Mountain Record of Zen Talks, 1988.
- Shunryu Suzuki, Zen Mind, Beginner's Mind. New York: Weatherhill, 1970.
- Kenneth Kraft, ed., Zen: Tradition and Transition
- Jon Covell and Yamada Sobin, Zen at Daitoku-ji. Tokyo: Kodansha, 1974.
- Irmgard Schloegl. The Zen Teaching of Rinzai. Berkeley: Shambhala, 1975.
- Zenkei Shibayama, Zen Comments on the Mumonkan, 1974.
- Steven Heine, Opening a Mountain: Koans of the Zen Masters (NY: Oxford, 2002)
- William Bodiford, Soto Zen in Medieval Japan, 1993.

- Miura Isshu and Ruth F. Sasaki, The Zen Koan. New York: Harcourt, 1965.
- Katsuki Sekida, trans., Two Zen Classics: Mumonkan & Hekiganroku, 1977.
- Thomas P. Kasulis, Zen Action/Zen Person. Honolulu: University of Hawaii Press, 1981.
- Masao Abe, Zen and Western Thought, 1985.
- Heinrich Dumoulin, Zen Buddhism: A History, 2 vols. New York: Macmillan, 1988, 1990.
- Norman Waddell, trans., The Essential Teachings of Zen Master Hakuin
- Frederick Franck, ed., The Buddha Eye: An Anthology of the Kyoto School, 1991.
- D.T. Suzuki, Manual of Zen Buddhism, 1934.
- D.T. Suzuki, Zen and Japanese Culture, 1959.

Discover more about Zen 2.0:
www.ZenRevolution.com

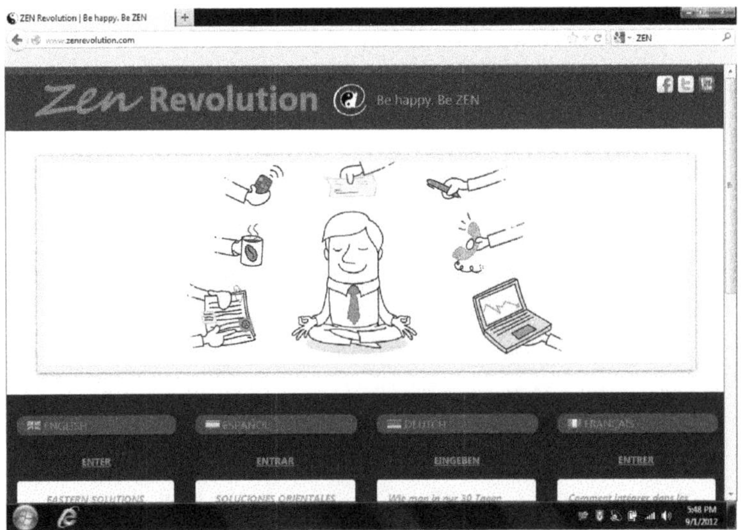

Welcome to Zen

www.ingramcontent.com/pod-product-compliance
Ingram Content Group UK Ltd.
Pitfield, Milton Keynes, MK11 3LW, UK
UKHW020240250726
13967UKWH00001B/468